CONTENTS

AMERICA, THROUGH ITS DIVISION VIA POLITICAL, SOCIAL, AND RACIAL MEANS, IS RAPIDLY APPROACHING COLLAPSE AND CIVIL WAR. THE GOVERNMENT'S INACTION TO ASSIST THE PEOPLE

LEADS TO A WEAKENING OF

THE COUNTRY AND DRIVES

THE PEOPLE TO TURN

AGAINST OUR NATION.

CORRUPTION RUNS

RAMPANT AMONG OUR

NATION WITHIN OUR STATE,

CITY, AND FEDERAL

GOVERNMENTS.

THE GOVERNMENT,
THOUGH KNOWING OF THE
ISSUE, OFTEN REFUSES TO
ADDRESS OR TURNS A
BLIND EYE TO THESE
PROBLEMS. THEY ALLOW
CORRUPTION TO FURTHER
BURROW INTO OUR
COUNTRY AND ENTRENCH

ITSELF, FEEDING OFF THE

LIFEBLOOD OF AMERICA,

THE AMERICAN PEOPLE.

CRIME DESTROYS OUR

CITIES AND ALLOWS FOR

THE INNOCENT TO BE

PREYED UPON, WITH THEIR

MONEY STOLEN AND OFTEN

LIVES ARE TAKEN.

Our borders are not
secured. Drugs flow
from our neighbors into
our cities, and then into
the hands of dealers
who sell to the addicts,
who then litter their
trash onto our streets.
This all puts the lives of

INNOCENT PEOPLE AT RISK,

INCLUDING CHILDREN. OUR

GOVERNMENT REFUSES TO

TAKE A FIRM HAND AT

CRUSHING THESE ISSUES,

AND LETS THE PEOPLE

SUFFER.

THE AMERICAN PUBLIC

ARE UNABLE TO AFFORD

FOOD, HEALTHCARE, AND

BILLS.

    THE GOVERNMENT AND

ITS BODIES, SUCH AS

CONGRESS, ARE SO DIVIDED

BY INFIGHTING THAT LAWS

THAT WOULD ULTIMATELY

HELP THE PEOPLE ARE

THROWN OUT AND LAWS

THAT HURT THE PEOPLE

ARE PASSED. THE

GOVERNMENT REFUSES TO

GIVE MORE RECOGNITION

TOWARDS THE SUFFERING

OF THE AMERICAN PEOPLE

AND FORCES THE PUBLIC TO

DEPEND ON THEMSELVES

AND THEIR FAMILIES TO

SURVIVE THROUGH A

RAPIDLY HOSTILE TURNING

NATION. WITHOUT A

STRONG AND CAPABLE

PRESIDENT WHO IS NOT

AFRAID TO STAND UP FOR

THE AMERICAN PEOPLE

AND COMBAT POLITICAL

CORRUPTION AND

INFIGHTING, AMERICA WILL

SOON BE PAST THE POINT

OF NO RETURN.

The Struggles I Faced

Ever since I grew up, I have been poor, even today I struggle to afford food. I have always struggled and still struggle to afford both bills and daily necessities. When I was

TWELVE, MY HOUSE AND

THE ENTIRE TOWN BURNT

DOWN IN THE CALDOR FIRE,

WITH BARELY ANY HOUSES

REMAINING. WE WERE

FORCED TO MOVE. THIS FIRE

COULD HAVE BEEN

STOPPED BUT THE

CALIFORNIAN

GOVERNMENT UNDER

GAVIN NEWSOM BEGAN

STRIPPING AWAY A KEY

LAYER OF DEFENSE FROM

FIRES BY SHUTTING DOWN

INMATE FIREFIGHTER

PROGRAMS. HE NOT ONLY

ENDED A REFORM

POSSIBILITY FOR

PRISONERS BUT ALSO

STRIPPED US, MY FAMILY,

PEOPLE, AND MY ENTIRE

COMMUNITY OF

PROTECTION.

I AND MY FAMILY THEN

LIVED WITH MY UNCLE AND

AUNT IN THEIR RV FOR

MONTHS UNTIL A VERY

SWEET COUPLE WHO I WILL

FOREVER BE THANKFUL FOR

TOOK US IN AND OFFERED

US HOUSING INSIDE A

RENTAL PROPERTY. WE

LIVED THERE UNTIL WE

MANAGED TO SCROUNGE UP

BARELY ENOUGH MONEY

FOR A HOUSE IN

Sacramento. With

California becoming

more expensive, soon

we, me and my family,

would not be able to

stay there anymore but

we also could not

afford to leave the

state. But also, I did not

WANT TO LEAVE IT. I HAVE
SEEN FIRSTHAND WHAT
HAS HAPPENED TO
CALIFORNIA AND I WANT TO
CHANGE IT. BUT CHANGE
REQUIRES THE BACKING OF
A LARGE NUMBER OF
PEOPLE. KNOWING THAT
THOSE WHO WISH TO

CHANGE THINGS OFTEN ARE

UNABLE TO DUE TO THE

DOMINANCE OF THE

REPUBLICAN AND

DEMOCRAT PARTIES, WE

NEED TO SPREAD OUR

WORD, OUR CALLS FOR

CHANGE. VOICES SOUND

LOUDER WHEN TOGETHER

THAN WHEN A SINGLE MAN

SHOUTS ALONE. WHEN THE

GOVERNMENT FAILS YOU,

YOU MUST RELY ON YOUR

FAMILY, NEIGHBORS, AND

COMMUNITY.

WHEN MY FAMILY,

SUCH AS MY UNCLE AND

BROTHER HAD SEVERE

MEDICAL ISSUES, MY UNCLE

WITH CANCER AND MY

BROTHER WITH ULCERS,

NOT ONLY DID THEY

SUFFER, BUT THEIR

FAMILIES ALSO SUFFERED.

MY UNCLE'S FAMILY WAS

FORCED TO PAY EXPENSIVE

BILLS FOR TREATMENT, AND

THEY STRUGGLED LONG

AFTER. MY FAMILY HAD TO

DO THE SAME AND WE STILL

HAD TO WORRY ABOUT

BEING ABLE TO PAY THE

BILLS YEARS AFTER. WITH

HEALTHCARE BEING SO

EXPENSIVE, IT MAKES MANY

FEAR OR NOT WANT TO GO

TO A HOSPITAL AS THEY

CANNOT AFFORD

TREATMENT. WHEN WE

FIRST MOVED INTO

SACRAMENTO, MY FAMILY'S

VEHICLES WERE ROBBED

MULTIPLE TIMES WITH

WINDOWS SHATTERED. ONE

OF THOSE TIMES, THEY

MANAGED TO BREAK INTO

MY BROTHER'S CAR AND

LEFT DRUGS ON OF THE

FRONT SEAT. WE CALLED

THE POLICE AND THEY SAID

THEY WOULD PATROL OUR

NEIGHBORHOOD, BUT WE

NEVER SAW A SINGLE

OFFICER PASS INTO OUR

NEIGHBORHOOD. WE STILL

HAD TO DEAL WITH THE

CRIMINALS ALONE. WE HAD

TO FEAR THAT ONE DAY OUR

NEIGHBORHOOD COULD GET

SHOT UP OR ONE DAY OUR

HOUSE COULD BE BROKEN

INTO BY ARMED CRIMINALS.

I KNOW PEOPLE WHO

WERE FALSELY ARRESTED

BY THE POLICE FOR

ACTIONS THEY DID NOT

COMMIT. I KNOW PEOPLE

WHO THE POLICE DETAINED

"ABUSE" WHEN REALLY,

THE PERSON THEY

DETAINED WERE THE ONES

BEING ABUSED. A FAMILY

FRIEND WAS ARRESTED

AND CHARGED WITH BEING

ABUSIVE WHEN THERE WAS

PROOF THAT HE WAS THE

ONE BEING ABUSED. HE

HAD BRUISES AND MARKS

ALL OVER HIM, BUT HE WAS

THE ONE PUNISHED, WHILST

HIS ABUSER TOOK HIS

CHILD. THE ABUSER HAD NO

MARKS ON HER AND SHE

WAS BELIEVED.

A MEMBER OF MY

FAMILY WAS FACING JAIL

TIME OVER AN ACT HE DID

NOT COMMIT. HE WAS

PULLED OVER FOR

"SPEEDING" WHEN, IN
REALITY, HE DID NOT GO
OVER THE SPEED LIMIT. NOT
ONLY DID THE POLICE'S
ACTIONS AGAINST HIM
AFFECT HIM, BUT IT ALSO
AFFECTED MY FAMILY. IT
ALSO PROVED TO ME THAT
THE NEED FOR REFORM

WAS AND STILL IS URGENT.

CORRUPT OFFICERS,

INCOMPETENT OFFICERS,

AND A BIASED JUSTICE

SYSTEM CREATES A

BREEDING GROUND FOR

ANTI-GOVERNMENT

SENTIMENT AND COSTS THE

GOOD OFFICERS, WHO

WORK FOR THE PEOPLE,

THE RESPECT AND HONOR

THEY DESERVE. I FEEL BAD

FOR THE OFFICERS WHO

ARE NOT CORRUPT AS THEY

ARE BUNCHED WITH THE

EVILNESS OF THE SYSTEM

AND ARE REAPING WHAT

THEY DID NOT SOW. WHEN

THE GOVERNMENT LOSES

THE TRUST OF THE PUBLIC,

AND THE JUSTICE SYSTEM

COLLAPSES UNDER THE

WEIGHT OF ITS OWN EVIL

AND BIASEDNESS, THIS

CAUSES THE COLLAPSE OF

SOCIETY. WITHOUT

SOCIETY, THE PEOPLE

SUFFER. WITHOUT SOCIETY,
INNOCENTS ARE
MASSACRED, AND CRIMINAL
GANGS TRANSFORM INTO
CRIMINAL ARMIES. THESE
CRIMINAL GANGS, IF THEY
ARE ALLOWED TO FULLY
TRANSFORM INTO AN ARMY
WILL BE ABLE TO ESTABLISH

CRIMINAL REPUBLICS,

WHICH WILL MASSACRE

INNOCENT AMERICANS

WHO WERE IN THE "WRONG

PLACE AT THE WRONG

TIME".

OUROBORISM AND

WHAT LED TO IT.

I FOUNDED THE IDEOLOGY OF OUROBORISM IN RESPONSE TO INCREASED INACTION BY THE GOVERNMENT TO COMBAT CORRUPTION, POLITICAL INFIGHTING,

CRIME, VIOLENCE, AND

INABILITY TO PROVIDE

PROPER SECURITY TO THE

AMERICAN PEOPLE. THIS

COMBINATION OF ISSUES

HAS LED TO THE DEATH OF

THOUSANDS ACROSS

AMERICA AND IF LEFT

UNCHECKED, WILL SPIRAL

INTO HUNDREDS OF

THOUSANDS IN A SHORT

PERIOD OF TIME.

OUROBORISM

PROMOTES THE

REFORMATION OF THE

GOVERNMENT BOTH ON A

FEDERAL AND STATE-WIDE

SCALE. IT CALLS FOR AN

END TO CORRUPTION,

INACTION, INCOMPETENCE,

AND EXPRESSES DESIRE

FOR A STRONG AND

CAPABLE LEADER WHERE

EVERY AMERICAN CAN

FINALLY PUT THEIR TRUST

INTO TO RESTORE ORDER,

PATRIOTISM, AND IMPROVE

WAY OF LIFE.

I HAVE HEARD MANY

STORIES OF THE JUSTICE

SYSTEM TARGETING PEOPLE

BASED ON PHYSICAL

DESCRIPTION AND

ALLOWING CRIMINALS TO

WALK FREE WITH LESS

THAN A SLAP ON THE WRIST

EVEN AFTER COMMITTING A

HORRIBLE CRIME SUCH AS

ABUSE, MURDER, AND THE

DIRECT TARGETING OF MEN,

WOMEN, AND CHILDREN IN

SEX CRIMES. A MAN FROM

ANCHORAGE, ALASKA,

NAMED JUSTIN SCHNEIDER

WAS ARRESTED FOR

STRANGLING A WOMAN

AFTER HAVING VIOLATED

HER IN A HORRIFIC WAY

AND THE JUDGE, NAMED

MICHEAL COREY, LET THE

MAN OFF WITH BARELY ANY

FORM OF PUNISHMENT.

JUSTICE WAS NOT

DELIVERED FOR THE VICTIM

WHO MUST NOW LIVE WITH

THE KNOWLEDGE THAT HER

VIOLATOR IS STILL

ALLOWED TO WALK FREELY

AMONG THE AMERICAN

PEOPLE.

I KNOW FRIENDS WHO

SUFFERED FROM HORRIBLE

ABUSE WHEN THEY WERE

YOUNGER. I SHALL NOT

NAME THEM OUT OF

RESPECT, BUT I WILL SHARE

THEIR EXPERIENCES. THEY

WERE MOLESTED. THEIR

ATTACKERS, WHICH WERE

FAMILY DID NOT FACE

PUNISHMENT.

My beloved mother,

when she was a little

girl, her stepfather

targeted and violated

her. He was given no

punishment. He was

allowed to walk free.

He lived freely. Justice

was not delivered. I will

FOREVER DESPISE THAT

MAN FOR WHAT HE DID TO

MY MOTHER. I WILL

FOREVER HATE THAT MAN

AND THOSE WHO TARGET

CHILDREN. I WILL FOREVER

WISH THE WORST UPON

THEM. IT PAINS ME THAT

THE JUSTICE SYSTEM DOES

NOT PUNISH THESE

"PEOPLE" AND GIVE THEM

WHAT THEY DESERVE. THEY

ARE INSTEAD ALLOWED TO

TARGET MORE CHILDREN

AFTER THEY SERVE THEIR

SENTENCES, WHICH ARE

OFTEN LESS THAN TEN

YEARS. OUR JUSTICE

SYSTEM THROUGH ITS

INACTION ALLOWS MORE

INNOCENT PEOPLE TO GET

HURT. MANY VICTIMS TAKE

THEIR OWN LIVES OR

SUFFER FROM EXTREMELY

SEVERE MENTAL ILLNESSES

FROM THESE ATTACKS.

LUCKILY MY MOTHER WAS

ALWAYS LOVING TO ALL

HER CHILDREN AND NEVER

LET HER PAST INTERFERE IN

OUR OR HER LIVES.

CORRUPTION DESTROYS

COUNTRIES AND LEADS TO

THE DEATHS OF

THOUSANDS OF INNOCENT

PEOPLE EVERY YEAR. THE

GOVERNMENT, THOUGH

FULLY CAPABLE OF

WORKING TO COMBAT IT,

INSTEAD REFUSES TO DO

SO. IT TURNS A BLIND EYE

WHILST THE ROOTS OF

CORRUPTION DIG DEEPER

AND DEEPER INTO SOCIETY,

FEEDING OFF THE

AMERICAN PEOPLE LIKE A
CANCER. IF THIS IS
ALLOWED TO CONTINUE, IT
WILL SOON BE TOO LATE TO
EFFECTIVELY COMBAT THE
ISSUE AND IT WILL CAUSE
MORE SUFFERING AND
DEATH THAN EVER BEFORE.

OUR POLICE, THOUGH

MEANT TO PROTECT THE

PEOPLE, ARE OFTEN RUN BY

CORRUPT CHIEFS OR

POSITIONS OCCUPIED BY

CORRUPT AND

INCOMPETENT OFFICERS.

THIS CREATES A SOCIETY

THAT IS UNABLE TO RELY ON

THEIR CITY, WHICH ALSO

CREATES A BREEDING

GROUND FOR MORE

CORRUPTION AND TURNS

THE PEOPLE AGAINST OUR

COUNTRY. AMERICA IS

MEANT TO BE A SHINING

BEACON OF DEMOCRACY

AND LIBERTY, BUT IT IS

UNABLE TO SHINE BRIGHTLY

WITH ALL THESE PROBLEMS

FESTERING.

THE NUMBER OF

UNEMPLOYED INDIVIDUALS

CONTINUES TO RISE ACROSS

THE U.S. BECAUSE OF AN

INCREASED RISK OF

ECONOMIC DOWNTURN AND

DEPRESSION. WITH THIS

LACK OF WORKERS AND

FAMILIES MAKING MONEY,

NOT ONLY DO FAMILIES

SUFFER, BUT OUR ECONOMY

DOES TOO. IF THIS RISE IN

UNEMPLOYMENT

CONTINUES, IT WILL RESULT

IN A TOTAL COLLAPSE OF

THE AMERICAN ECONOMY

AND LEAD TO THE

FRACTURING OF OUR

UNION.

HOMELESSNESS

CONTINUES TO EXPAND

ACROSS AMERICA AS A

RESULT OF EXPENSIVE

BILLS, INCREASING RENTS,

AND UNEMPLOYMENT.

ENTIRE FAMILIES ARE LEFT

ON THE STREETS TO SUFFER

AND ARE UNABLE TO

AFFORD HOMES DUE TO OUR

UNSTABLE HOUSING

MARKET. ACCORDING TO

THE COUNTY OF LOS

ANGELAS, OVER 1,000

PEOPLE EXPERIENCING

HOMELESSNESS DIED. IT IS

ESTIMATED THAT EVERY

DAY, TWENTY HOMELESS

PEOPLE DIE. THIS MEANS

THAT EVERY YEAR, AT

LEAST 7,300 AMERICANS

DIE BECAUSE OF

HOMELESSNESS.

HOMELESSNESS ALSO

LEADS TO ANOTHER MAJOR

ISSUE: ADDICTION.

ADDICTION WREAKS

HAVOC ON THE AMERICAN

POPULATION. OUR CITIES,

ONCE BEAUTIFUL, ARE NOW

FULL OF LITTERED

GARBAGE SUCH AS

NEEDLES AND OTHER ITEMS

USED BY ADDICTS TO

FULFILL THEIR NEED FOR A

HIGH. ACCORDING TO THE

NATIONAL SURVEY ON

DRUG USE AND HEALTH,

16.7% OF AMERICANS,

WITH THE LOWEST AGE

COUNTED BEING TWELVE,

HAVE SUFFERED OR ARE

CURRENTLY SUFFERING

FROM ADDICTION. OVER

20,000 BABIES ARE BORN

EACH YEAR THAT SUFFER

FROM DEPENDENCY ON

DRUGS DUE TO THE ACTIONS

OF THEIR PARENTS. OUR

STREETS AND PARKS ARE

NOT SAFE FOR CHILDREN

ANYMORE DUE TO THE VAST

NUMBER OF NEEDLES AND

OTHER ITEMS THAT ADDICTS

LEAVE AROUND, PUTTING

THE LIVES OF CHILDREN,

ANIMALS, AND ADULTS AT

RISK. EVERY YEAR, AT

LEAST 800,000

AMERICANS RECEIVE A

NEEDLESTICK INJURY FROM

USED DRUG SYRINGES.

MANY OF THESE VICTIMS

WILL OFTEN CONTRACT

DISEASES THAT CANNOT BE

CURED OR WILL FOREVER

LEAVE THEIR LIVES IN RUIN.

DRUG ADDICTS WITHIN OUR

COUNTRY ARE ENABLED AS

STATE GOVERNMENTS,

INSTEAD OF COMBATING

THE ISSUE, FUEL IT BY

REFUSING TO MOVE USERS

INTO REHABILITATION. THE

USERS UTILIZE THE

GOVERNMENTS

IRRESPONSIBILITY TO

FREELY USE AND PURCHASE

DRUGS IN THE OPEN. MOST

OF THESE ADDICTS,

INSTEAD OF TURNING TO

RECEIVE HELP, REFUSE TO

DO SO AND TURN TO

VIOLENCE WHEN SOMEONE

EVEN TALKS ABOUT

REHABILITATION. THE WAR

ON DRUGS FAILED A LONG

TIME AGO. THE WAR TO

PROVIDE COMFORT AND

HELP TO THE AMERICAN

PEOPLE TO COMBAT THE

RAPID GROWTH IN CRIMINAL

GANGS WHICH TRAFFIC

DRUGS WAS A LOSS. THE

GOVERNMENT, THROUGH

USING PEACE, PROVED

THAT THEY WERE WEAK IN
THEIR ABILITIES TO DEFEND
THE AMERICAN PEOPLE
FROM INTERNAL ISSUES,
AND ONLY USE STRENGTH
ON THE OUTSIDE. OUR
STRENGTHS SHOULDN'T
JUST BE USED ON THE
OUTSIDE, BUT SHOULD ALSO

BE USED ON THE INSIDE TO

BRING ABOUT AN END TO

THE IMMENSE CRIMINAL

UNDERGROUND.

Across America, we

MUST FEAR GOING OUTSIDE

OR GOING TO BUY

GROCERIES DUE TO THE

HIGH VIOLENCE RATE

WITHIN OUR CITIES. OUR

CHILDREN MUST FEAR

GOING TO SCHOOL DUE TO

THE HIGH RISK OF

SHOOTINGS. PSYCHOPATHS

AND SOCIOPATHS WALK

FREELY EVERY DAY AND AT

ANY POINT, THEY CAN SNAP

OR SIMPLY DECIDE TO

STRIKE AN INNOCENT AND

MURDER THEM. 27% OF

HOMICIDES ARE CAUSED BY

PSYCHOPATHS AND OVER

70% OF CRIMINALS ARE

SOCIOPATHS. DYLAN

STORM ROOF, THE MAN

WHO COMMITTED THE

HORRIFIC CRIME OF THE

Charleston Church

Shooting, is a sociopath.

Nine people were killed

that day, and we haven't

learned. Another

shooting, the Buffalo

Shooting in 2022,

resulted in the death of

ten innocent people.

PAYTON S. GENDRON SHOT

UP A BLACK COMMUNITY

OVER HIS HATRED. HE

OFTEN MADE "JOKES"

ABOUT WANTING TO COMMIT

MURDER-SUICIDE OR MASS

SHOOTING WHEN HE WAS IN

HIGH SCHOOL, AND YET

NOTHING WAS DONE EVEN

WHEN HE WAS BROUGHT IN

FOR A PSYCHIATRIC

EVALUATION. WE ALLOW

THESE PEOPLE TO

CONTINUE WALKING THE

STREETS WHEN THEY POSE

A RISK TO THE SAFETY OF

US ALL, ESPECIALLY OUR

CHILDREN. JULY 4TH, A DAY

MEANT TO SYMBOLIZE OUR

DECLARATION AS A FREE

NATION, A DAY MEANT TO

BE JOYFUL, OFTEN INSTEAD

TURNED INTO TRAGEDIES,

AS MONSTERS USE THE

LARGE CROWDS TO PLAY

OUT THEIR FANTASIES AND

COMMIT HORRIFIC

SHOOTINGS ON INNOCENT

PEOPLE. IN 2023, TWENTY-

TWO SHOOTINGS OCCURRED

DURING INDEPENDENCE

DAY CELEBRATIONS

ACROSS THE COUNTRY.

DURING A SINGLE

CELEBRATION, TWENTY

PEOPLE WERE KILLED AND

126 WERE INJURED. THE

COLUMBINE SHOOTERS

BOTH SUFFERED FROM

PSYCHOPATHY, AND THAT

RESULTED IN THEM

MURDERING FIFTEEN

INNOCENT PEOPLE, MOST

BEING KIDS. JUSTICE WAS

NEVER OFFICIALLY SERVED

FOR THE PARENTS OF

THOSE WHO WERE LOST.

RETIRED CALIFORNIAN

POLICE CHIEF, ANDREAS

PROBST, WAS STRUCK BY

TWO TEENAGERS IN 2023.

HE WAS AN INNOCENT MAN

ENJOYING A BIKE RIDE, AND

ON WHAT WAS SUPPOSED

TO BE A RELAXING MOMENT,

TURNED INTO A TRAGEDY.

HE HAD A FAMILY AND HIS

ATTACKERS LAUGHED

DURING THE TRIAL. THEY

MOCKED THE FAMILY. THE

TEENAGERS WHO KILLED

MISTER PROBST: JESUS

AYALA AND JZAMIR KEYS

VERY CLEARLY HAVE

PSYCHOPATHY. THEY LACK

ANY SORT OF CARE FOR

THOSE AROUND THEM AND

ENJOY HARMING OTHERS.

WE MUST PREVENT MORE

INNOCENT AMERICANS,

INCLUDING CHILDREN FROM

BEING KILLED BY PEOPLE

WHO LACK CARE FOR THEIR

FELLOW HUMAN BEINGS.

THE STATE

GOVERNMENTS, THROUGH

THEIR INACTION,

INCOMPETENCY, AND LACK

OF CARE FOR THE PUBLIC

HAVE CREATED A CORRUPT

AND UNSTABLE SYSTEM.

WITHIN WASHINGTON,

DRUG ADDICTS AND

SQUATTERS, WHO COST THE

TAXPAYERS MONEY, ARE

ALLOWED TO DO WHATEVER

THEY DESIRE. SQUATTERS

ARE ALLOWED TO OCCUPY

HOMES OF PEOPLE AND ARE

PROTECTED BY THE LAW

AND ARE ABLE TO CLAIM

OWNERSHIP OF THE

PROPERTY USING ADVERSE

POSSESSION AS

JUSTIFICATION. WHEN

HOMEOWNERS TRY TO EVICT

THESE SQUATTERS, THEY

ARE OFTEN THE ONES WHO

GET PUNISHED, NOT THE

SQUATTERS. IN NEW YORK,

A 52-YEAR-OLD MOTHER

WAS KILLED BY TWO

SQUATTERS. THESE

SQUATTERS THEN STOLE

HER CREDIT CARDS AND

WENT ON A SHOPPING

SPREE WITH HER MONEY.

HER BODY WAS FOUND

DUMPED INSIDE A DUFFLE

BAG WITH CORDS WRAPPED

AROUND HER NECK AND

LEFT TO ROT. SQUATTERS

ARE A MAJOR THREAT TO

SOCIETY AND THE

GOVERNMENTS EXPECT US

TO LET THEM OCCUPY OUR

HOMES AND

NEIGHBORHOODS. THEY
EXPECT US TO SIT AND
WATCH AS OUR TOWNS GET
DESTROYED BY OCCUPIERS
WHO ARE A RISK TO
EVERYONE AROUND THEM.

THE AVERAGE
AMERICAN IS NO LONGER
SAFE WITHIN THEIR CITIES

DUE TO THE RAPID GROWTH

AND INCREASE IN CRIME

ACROSS OUR COUNTRY.

CRIMINAL GANGS MURDER

AND LOOT ACROSS OUR

TOWNS AND DUE TO AVID

CORRUPTION AMONGST CITY

LEADERSHIP, COMBINED

WITH DISCONNECTION AND

A LACK OF KNOWLEDGE ON

THE LIVES OF THE POOR,

THEY ARE ALLOWED TO RUN

AS THE GOVERNMENTS,

INSTEAD OF CUTTING THE

ROOT, THE POVERTY OF THE

LOWER-CLASS

NEIGHBORHOODS, ONLY

TARGET THE FRUITS, THE

GANGS, WHICH WILL GROW

BACK IN EVEN LARGER

NUMBERS.

PATRIOTS ARE NO

LONGER ABLE TO EXPRESS

THEIR LOVE FOR AMERICA

WITHOUT BEING MOCKED.

OUR SYMBOLS OF NATIONAL

UNITY AND INDEPENDENCE

ARE DESTROYED AND

BURNED. OUR FLAG, WHICH

REPRESENTS FREEDOM AND

DEMOCRACY, IS BURNED,

DEFECATED, AND URINATED

ON, AND THOSE WHO

DESTROY IT ARE ABLE TO

FREELY DO SO. THEY SHOUT

THAT AMERICA WAS NEVER

GREAT, THEY SHOUT THAT

THOSE WHO LOVE AMERICA

ARE FASCISTS. THEY SHOUT

THAT THOSE WHO FEEL

PATRIOTIC ARE NAZIS. WE

CAN NO LONGER FEEL LOVE

FOR OUR COUNTRY

WITHOUT BEING TARGETED,

HARASSED, AND MOCKED.

OUR CURRENT

GOVERNMENT DOES NOT

HELP THE SITUATION

EITHER WITH ITS ACTIONS.

THE UTILIZATION OF CALLS

FOR VIOLENCE BY SOME

POLITICIANS CAUSES EVEN

MORE DIVISION AMONG THE

PEOPLE AS THEY DEMAND

THAT WE TURN ON THOSE

AROUND US TO ACHIEVE

POLITICAL AIMS. I DESCRIBE

ALL THESE ISSUES UNDER

TWO WORDS: DECAYING

DEMOCRACY. OUR COUNTRY

IS UNDER A DECAYING

DEMOCRACY AND SOON IT

WILL HAVE ROTTED SO FAR

IT CANNOT BE FIXED.

WITHOUT CHANGE, OUR

COUNTRY WILL RETURN TO

THE SOIL, BUT WILL BE

UNABLE TO SPROUT

ANOTHER TREE OF LIBERTY.

IF WE ALLOW OUR COUNTRY

TO CONTINUE FALLING

FURTHER AND FURTHER,

OUTSIDE THREATS WILL

92

TAKE OUR PLACE AS A

GLOBAL POWER AND WILL

STRIP THE WORLD OF

DEMOCRACY AND

FREEDOM.

<u>*An Ouroborist Future*</u>

The future of the United States, as of now, is not in good hands. It is in unstable and shaky hands, which threaten to drop the future to the ground, where it, having already

FACED DAMAGE, WILL BE

LEFT TO FURTHER ROT AND

WITHER. OUROBORISM

PROMISES TO ENSURE THE

FUTURE IS NOT DROPPED,

AND THAT THE HANDS THAT

CURRENTLY GRASP IT ARE

CHANGED TOWARDS A NEW

PAIR WHICH WILL USE

STRENGTH TO PREVENT

COLLAPSE AND LOSS.

DECAY CAN ONLY BE

REVERSED THROUGH A

COMPLETE CHANGE, AND

THUS, OUR CURRENT

DEMOCRACY WILL BE

SWAPPED FOR A NEW ONE,

WHERE FREEDOM AND

LIBERTY WILL BE

RESTORED. OUR FOUNDING

FATHERS WILL NO LONGER

NEED TO WORRY ABOUT

THEIR COUNTRY FROM

BEYOND THE GRAVE, AND

CAN BE ASSURED THAT

PEACE, ORDER, AND THE

PEOPLE'S SAFETY HAS

BEEN ASSURED.

OUROBORISM IS BUILT

ON THE PRINCIPLE OF UNITY

OF THE AMERICAN PEOPLE,

FULLY REMOVING THE LINES

OF DIVISION BETWEEN US

SUCH AS RACIAL,

POLITICAL, AND SOCIAL.

OUROBORISM, THROUGH

THE PARTY AS DESCRIBED

LATER, SEEKS TO UNITE

PEOPLE FROM ACROSS THE

NATION UNDER ONE

BANNER, TO FINALLY BRING

ABOUT AN END TO THE

PEOPLE'S SEPARATION.

THROUGH UNITY OUR

PEOPLE WILL PROSPER AND

THROUGH UNITY CAN

SOCIAL ORDER BE

RESTORED AND OUR SPOT

AS A GLOBAL POWER

REMAIN. THROUGH

SEPARATION WE ARE

ABUSED AND THROUGH

SEPARATION OUR POSITION

AS A POWER IS

THREATENED AS RIVALS

USE OUR WEAKNESS TO

CREATE A SENSE OF

DISTRUST AROUND OUR

ALLIES. THE ASPECT OF

HATRED BETWEEN RACES

CREATES A WEAK NATION.

AS LINCOLN STATED, "A

HOUSE DIVIDED CANNOT

STAND". WITHOUT OUR

DIVERSITY, WE WOULD NOT

STAND AS A SHINING

BEACON OF LIBERTY.

WITHOUT OUR DIVERSITY,

THE POEM ENGRAVED ON A

PLAQUE ON THE STATUE OF

LIBERTY WOULD NOT STAND

TRUE. THE NEW COLOSSUS,

A POEM WRITTEN BY EMMA

LAZARUS DESCRIBES THE

UNITED STATES AS A HOME

FOR THE UNWANTED, A

HAVEN FOR THE LOST AND

POOR, AND A SAFE PLACE

FOR THE MASSES YEARNING

FOR FREEDOM.

THE NEW COLOSSUS

Emma Lazarus

"Not like the brazen giant of Greek fame, with conquering limbs astride from land to land; Here at our sea-washed, sunset gates shall stand, mighty

WOMAN WITH A TORCH, WHOSE FLAME IS THE IMPRISONED LIGHTNING, AND HER NAME MOTHER OF EXILES. FROM HER BEACON-HAND GLOWS WORLD-WIDE WELCOME; HER MILD EYES COMMAND. THE AIR-BRIDGED HARBOR THAT

TWIN CITIES FRAME. "'KEEP,
ANCIENT LANDS, YOUR
STORIED POMP!'" CRIES SHE
WITH SILENT LIPS. "GIVE ME
YOUR TIRED, YOUR POOR,
YOUR HUDDLED MASSES
YEARNING TO BREATHE
FREE, THE WRETCHED
REFUSE OF YOUR TEEMING

SHORE. SEND THESE, THE HOMELESS, TEMPEST-TOSSED TO ME, I LIFT MY LAMP BESIDE THE GOLDEN DOOR!"'"

A BEAUTIFUL POEM REPRESENTING THE UNITED STATES AS WHAT IT WAS ALWAYS MEANT TO BE, A

HAVEN FOR THE EXILES,

FOR THE SCARED, AND FOR

THOSE WHO DO NOT

BELONG ANYWHERE ELSE.

THROUGH OUR DIVISION, WE

LOSE THIS MEANING

THROUGH A LAYER OF

HATRED AND VIOLENCE.

WITH OUROBORISM,

THROUGH ITS GOAL TO

PROVIDE UNITY FOR EVERY

AMERICAN, CAN THE

PEOPLE WITH NOWHERE

ELSE TO GO TRULY FEEL

WHAT BELONGING FEELS

LIKE. SHALL EVERY

OUROBORIST USE THE NEW

COLOSSUS AS A GUIDE TO

PRESERVE UNITY AND

THROUGH PRESERVING

UNITY, PRESERVE THE

UNITED STATES. EVERY

AMERICAN OF EVERY RACE

AND CLASS WILL BE GIVEN

A CHANCE BY A NEWLY

FORGED GOVERNMENT TO

REBUILD AMERICA, BE IT

THROUGH THE

ESTABLISHMENT OF NEW

BUSINESSES OR THE

ASSURANCE OF A STABLE

CAREER.

Ouroborism, as an

ideology, desires to

reconstruct the

government towards

ONE THAT ACTUALLY

SHOWS CARE FOR THE

AMERICAN PEOPLE. IT

DESIRES TO FORM A

STRONG LEADERSHIP WITH

A LEADER WHO IS NOT

AFRAID TO DO WHAT MUST

BE DONE TO ENSURE

PEACE, SAFETY, AND ORDER

IS ASSURED DOMESTICALLY.

IN OUR FUTURE, THE

GOVERNMENT WILL BE

REBUILT. NO MORE WILL

CORRUPTION REIGN

SUPREME AND THE

INCOMPETENT REMAIN IN

THEIR POSITIONS OF HIGH

POWER. THOSE WHO PREY

ON THE INNOCENT WILL

FACE WHAT IS DUE TO

THEM. IN OUR FUTURE, THE

JUSTICE SYSTEM WILL BE

REFORMED, CREATING A

NEW SYSTEM WHICH THE

AMERICAN PUBLIC CAN

TRUST. JUDGES WHO ONLY

SERVE THEMSELVES AND

NOT THE PEOPLE WILL BE

REPLACED BY JUDGES WHO

WORK TOWARDS THE GOAL

OF PROTECTING THE PUBLIC

BY ANY MEANS NECESSARY.

GONE WILL BE THE DAYS OF

PREDATORS AND

MURDERERS BEING

ALLOWED TO ATTACK

ANOTHER INNOCENT BEING

AND A NEW ERA OF

NATIONAL SAFETY WILL BE

USHERED IN.

HOMELESSNESS WILL

BECOME A THING OF THE

PAST. IN THE EYES OF

OUROBORISM, EVERY

AMERICAN DESERVES

SHELTER. UNDER AN

OUROBORIST GOVERNMENT,

AFFORDABLE HOUSING

COMPLEXES WILL BE BUILT.

UNLIKE THE NEGLECTED

AFFORDABLE COMPLEXES

OF THE PAST, THESE NEW

COMPLEXES WOULD BE

MAINTAINED BY

GOVERNMENT APPOINTED

WORKERS AND OFFICIALS.

IN ORDER TO PREVENT

SUFFERING AND THE

FORMATION OF CRIMINAL

GANGS WITHIN THESE

COMMUNITIES, THE NEW

GOVERNMENT FORGED BY

THE IDEOLOGY OF

OUROBORISM WILL PROVIDE

EMPLOYMENT

OPPORTUNITIES TO

RESIDENTS. AFFORDABLE

SCHOOLING AND REFORM

EFFORTS WILL BE FUNDED

AND SPONSORED BY THE

GOVERNMENT TO PROVIDE

EQUAL OPPORTUNITIES TO

CHILDREN OF ALL AGES,

CLASSES, AND RACES.

IN AN OUROBORIST

SOCIETY, PATRIOTISM WILL

ONCE AGAIN BECOME

POPULAR. THE DISSENT

SPREAD AMONG OUR

NATION BY ACTIVIST

GROUPS WHO DO NOT HAVE

THE BEST INTEREST OF THE

PEOPLE IN THEIR MIND WILL

NOT BE TOLERATED. THE

DESTRUCTION OF NATIONAL

SYMBOLS OF OUR

INDEPENDENCE WILL BE

HALTED BY THE

GOVERNMENT. IF WE

ALLOW THESE GROUPS TO

CONTINUE DESTROYING OUR

HISTORIC SYMBOLS, WHAT

WILL WE HAVE LEFT TO

LEARN FROM? WHAT WILL

WE HAVE LEFT TO PRAISE?

IF WE LET THEM CONTINUE

TO CHANGE OUR SOCIETY,

ARE WE TRULY THE

COUNTRY WE WERE MEANT

TO BE? OUROBORISM,

THROUGH ITS PROMISE TO

RESTORE ORDER AND

PATRIOTISM TO OUR

COUNTRY, ALSO PROMISES

TO ENSURE THE

PROTECTION OF OUR

NATIONAL SYMBOLS BY ANY

MEANS NECESSARY.

PATRIOTS WILL BE ABLE TO

OPENLY EXPRESS THEIR

LOVE FOR OUR COUNTRY

WITHOUT BEING ATTACKED.

OUR NATION WILL BECOME

A BEACON OF GREATNESS

AND INTEGRITY, BUT IF WE

CONTINUE TO ALLOW

PEOPLE TO BURN OUR

FLAGS AND TOPPLE OUR

STATUES, WE WILL

CRUMBLE AS A PEOPLE.

ADDICTS AND DEALERS,

WHO DESTROY OUR CITIES

BY LITTERING THEIR

GARBAGE AND ATTACKING

THE INNOCENT WILL NO

LONGER BE TOLERATED.

THE STATE GOVERNMENTS

WHICH PREVIOUSLY

ALLOWED THEM TO

CONTINUE THEIR CRIMES OF

USING, DEALING, AND

VANDALIZING WILL BE

FORCED TO TAKE ACTION.

WITH A NEW OUROBORIST

GOVERNMENT PROMISING

TO CREATE A NEW BASE OF

LEADERSHIP WITH A

STRONG AND CAPABLE

LEADER, THESE GOALS WILL

BECOME MORE POSSIBLE AS

TIME GOES ON. DEALERS

WILL BE STOPPED AND THE

FLOW OF DRUGS INTO OUR

NATION WILL BE HALTED BY

THE SECURING OF OUR

BORDERS. HARSH

PUNISHMENT IS NEEDED TO

SEND A MESSAGE THAT WE

WILL NO LONGER ACCEPT

AND TOLERATE CRIMINALS

AMONG OUR SOCIETY, AND

THAT WE WILL PROTECT

OUR PEOPLE AT ANY COST.

OUR STREETS WILL BE
CLEANED PERMANENTLY,
AND ADDICTS WILL BE PUT
INTO REHABILITATION. IT IS
FOR THE BEST THAT WE
TREAT THEM BEFORE ITS
TOO LATE, AS ONCE ITS TOO
LATE, THEY WILL NEVER BE
ABLE TO STOP THEIR SELF-

INFLICTED DESTRUCTION

AND THE DESTRUCTION OF

OUR COUNTRY.

Political infighting

among our government,

both federal and state

bodies, prevents the

creation of a truly

unified nation. As

STATED, MANY TIMES,

DIVISION CREATES A

BREEDING GROUND FOR

CRIME, ANTI-GOVERNMENT

SENTIMENT, TRUST ISSUES,

AND WEAKNESS. THE

FEDERAL GOVERNMENT,

WITH IT BEING DOMINATED

BY THOSE WHO DO NOT

KNOW HOW IT FEELS TO BE

APART OF THE MAJORITY

CLASSES, SUCH AS THE

POOR AND STRUGGLING

ARE TRUSTED TO PASS

LAWS AND REPRESENT THE

POOR, WHEN INSTEAD, THE

POOR SHOULD BE TRUSTED

TO ACCURATELY

REPRESENT THE POOR, AND

THE RICH TO REPRESENT

THE RICH. NO WONDER

THAT OUR CONCERNS, THE

PEOPLE, THE MAJORITY

CLASSES ARE IGNORED AND

NEGLECTED. WE DO NOT

HAVE A SYSTEM WHERE WE

CAN PROPERLY GET OUR

DEMANDS OUT. THE POOR

HAVE ALWAYS BEEN

NEGLECTED AND THIS IS

WHAT ALLOWED GANGS TO

FORM AND TAKE

ADVANTAGE OF THE

PEOPLE. THE GOVERNMENT,

INSTEAD OF STRIKING THE

ROOT, ONLY STRUCK THE

INDIVIDUAL LEAVES. SURE,

THEY TOOK A FEW, BUT

LEAVES GROW BACK. THE

GOVERNMENT ALLOWED

THE TREE OF CRIME TO

CONTINUE GROWING AND

SIMPLY WATCHED AS IT

TOOK NUTRIENTS FROM

OTHERS, THE AMERICAN

PEOPLE AND DID NOTHING.

OUROBORISM ALWAYS

SEEKS TO STRIKE THE ROOT

OF THE ISSUE, NEVER THE

LEAVES OR BRANCHES. IT

ALWAYS SEEKS TO DESTROY

THE CAUSE BEFORE

STRIKING THE EFFECT.

WITHOUT DESTROYING THE

CAUSE, THE EFFECT GROWS

AND GROWS AND GETS

HARDER TO DESTROY.

THE UNITED STATES

DESERVES A CHANCE TO

CHANGE, A CHANCE TO

REFORM AND BE REBUILT.

OUROBORISM SEEKS TO

REVITALIZE THE NATION,

REFORM THE NUMEROUS

SYSTEMS, AND PROTECT

THE PEOPLE FROM

INTERNAL AND EXTERNAL

THREATS.

THE FUTURE OF

OUROBORISM AND THE

FUTURE OF AMERICA

COINCIDE. OUROBORISM

DEPENDS ON THE PEOPLE

TO ACHIEVE ITS GOALS AND

AMERICA DEPENDS ON

OUROBORISM TO BRING

CHANGE AND REVITALIZE

THE NATION.